FLORENTINE EMBROIDERY

A McMinn
(compiler)

δελος

Chairseat

MATERIALS: Chairseat approximately: 48 cm × 40 cm × 48 cm. Adjust quantities to suit individual requirements.

Anchor Tapisserie Wool (10 m skein): 27 skeins terra cotta 0868; 3 skeins each chestnut 0352, dusky pink 069, 068; 2 skeins apricot 0743.

70 cm single thread tapestry canvas, 18 threads (17 holes) to 2,5 cm, 68 cm wide. Tapestry frame with 68 cm tapes. *Milward* International Range tapestry needle No. 18.

INSTRUCTIONS: Mark the centre of canvas lengthwise and widthwise with a line of basting stitches. With a pencil mark the outline of the chairseat measurements centrally on the canvas, using the basting stitches as a guide and making sure the horizontal front and back edges match the straight weave of the canvas. Mount the canvas on frame with outline of chairseat side edges to tapes. *Diagram 1* gives a little more than one quarter of the cental motif and also shows the arrangement of the stitches on the threads of the canvas, represented by the background lines. The design is worked over 8 canvas threads throughout. The large black arrows indicate the centre of the chairseat and should coincide with the basting stitches.

Commence the design centrally and work the foundation rows following *diagram 1*. Work the numbered sections with the appropriate colour. To complete the motif work other three quarters to correspond, then continue working the remaining outer area to the pencil outline shape in 0868 only. A neat outer edge is achieved by adjusting the length of the stitches to fit the pencil outline shape.

TO MAKE UP: Place the embroidery centrally on the chair pad. Fold the canvas back and secure in position on the underside with upholstery tacks.

Diagram 2 shows a single row of stitches over 8 canvas threads.

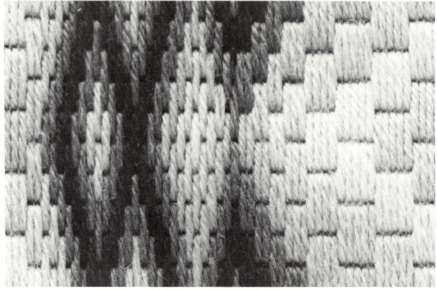

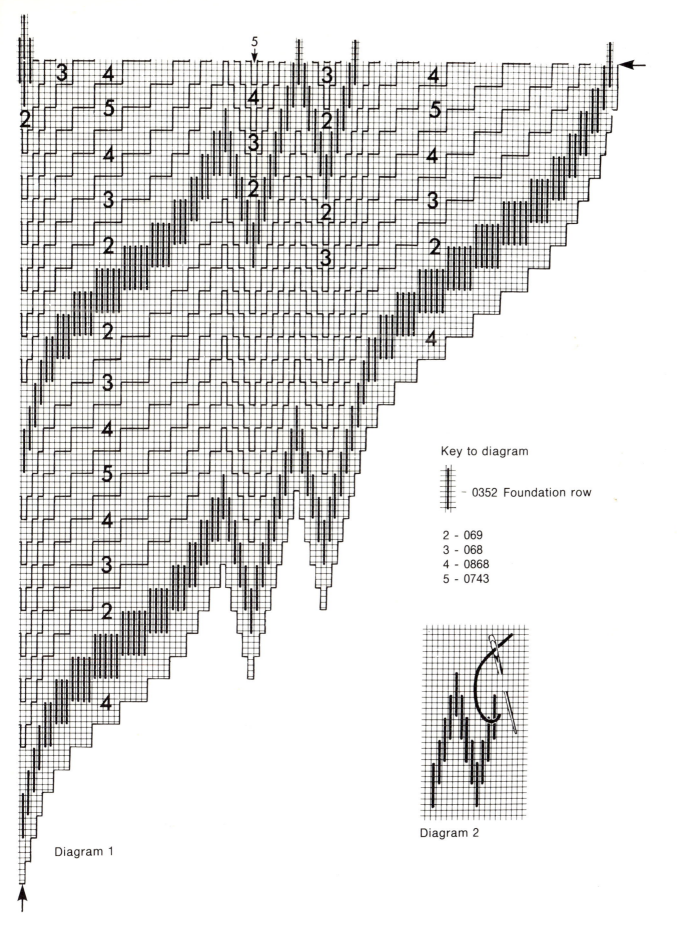

Key to diagram

‖ – 0352 Foundation row

2 - 069
3 - 068
4 - 0868
5 - 0743

Diagram 1

Diagram 2

3

Stooltop

MATERIALS: Stooltop 41 × 33 cm. Adjust quantities to suit individual requirements. Anchor Tapisserie Wool (10 m skein): 4 skeins each raspberry 024, muscat green 0278, terra cotta 0337, brick red 0339, cinnamon 0358, olive green 0422, muscat green 0843 and 3 skeins raspberry 023.

40 cm single thread canvas 18 threads (17 holes) to 2,5 cm, 68 cm wide. Tapestry frame with 68 cm tapes. Milward International Range tapestry needle No. 18.

INSTRUCTIONS: Mark the centre of canvas lengthwise and width-wise with a line of basting stitches.

Mount canvas on frame, long edges to tapes. *Diagram 1* gives motifs A and B, centre indicated by black arrows which should coincide with the basting stitches. *Diagram 1* also shows the arrangement of the stitches on the threads of the canvas represented by the back-ground lines. The design is worked throughout over 6 canvas threads, but it will be necessary to work part stitches to fit the outline shape. The *layout diagram* gives a little more than the left half of the design, centre indicated by broken lines which should coincide with the basting stitches. The shaded area repre-

sents motifs A and B given in *diagram 1*.

Commence the design centrally and work the foundation row following *diagram 1* and key to diagram. To complete the left half repeat these motifs following *layout diagram*. To complete design work the right half to correspond.

TO MAKE UP: Place the embroidery centrally on the stool pad. Fold the canvas back and secure in position on the underside with upholstery tacks.
Diagram 2 shows a single row of stitches over 6 threads.

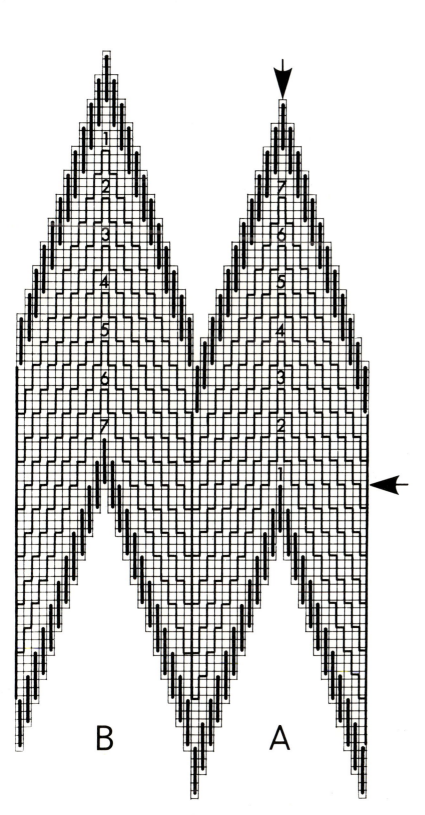

B   **A**

Diagram 1

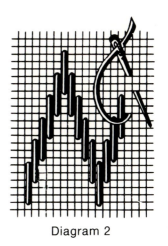

Diagram 2

Key to diagram

  – 0358 – Foundation row

1 – 0339

2 – 0337

3 – 024

4 – 023

5 – 027

6 – 0422

7 – 0843

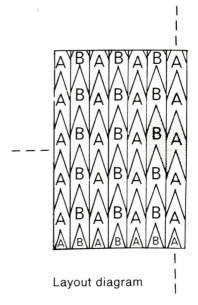

Layout diagram

Cushion

MATERIALS: Anchor Tapisserie Wool (10 m skein): 8 skeins oyster 0392; 6 skeins salmon pink 0892; 4 skeins each raspberry 023, salmon pink 0336, oyster 0981 and tapestry pink 067.

50 cm single thread tapestry canvas, 18 threads (17 holes) to 2,5 cm, 68 cm wide. 50 cm matching medium weight fabric for backing 91 cm wide. Cushion pad to fit. Tapestry frame. Milward International Range tapestry needle No. 18.

INSTRUCTIONS: Mark the centre of canvas lengthwise and widthwise with a line of basting stitches. Mount canvas on frame with long edges to tapes. *Diagram 1* gives an eighth of the design, centre indicated by black arrows which should coincide with the basting stitches. The background lines on the diagram represent the threads of the canvas. The design is worked throughout over 6 canvas threads expect in those areas where the length of stitch has been adjusted to fit the diagonal corners and give a neat outer edge.

Commence the design centrally with the foundation row and work following *diagram 1* and key for embroidery. To complete one quarter, work in reverse from vertical black arrow. To complete the design turn canvas and work other three quarters in the same way.

TO MAKE UP: Trim canvas to within 1,5 cm of embroidery. Cut a piece from backing fabric the same size. Place back and front right sides together and stitch close to the embroidery, leaving an opening on one side for pad insertion. Turn to right side, insert pad and sew opening. *Diagram 2* shows a single row of stitches over 6 threads.

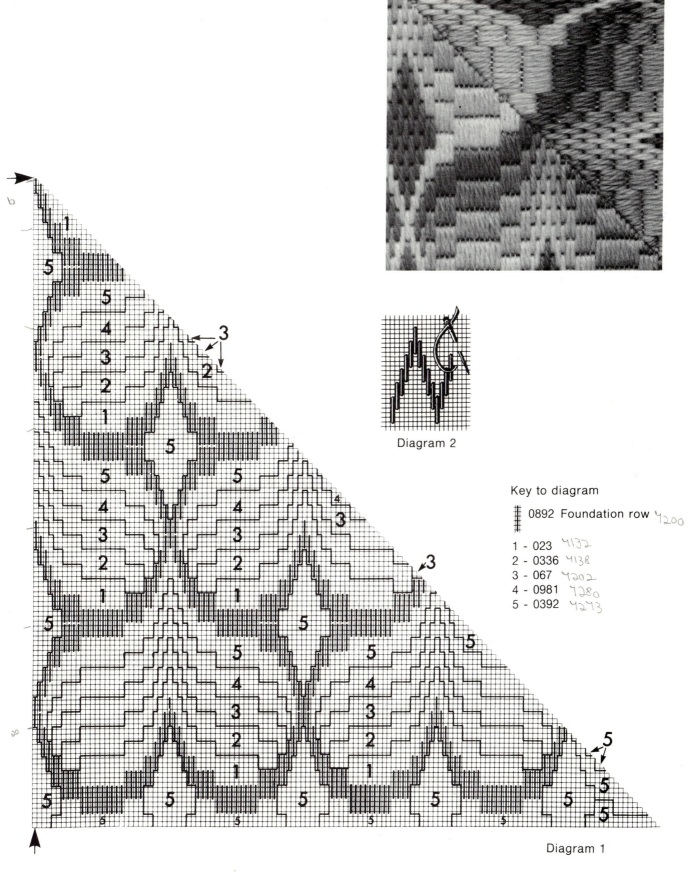

Diagram 2

Key to diagram

0892 Foundation row 4200

1 - 023 4132
2 - 0336 4138
3 - 067 4202
4 - 0981 4280
5 - 0392 4273

Diagram 1

7

Cushion

MATERIALS: Anchor Stranded Cotton: 7 skeins olive green 0842; 4 skeins cream 02. Use 6 strands throughout.

Anchor Tapisserie Wool (10 m skein); 14 skeins sage green 0842; 6 skeins each cream 0732, white 0402, and olive green 0422, 50 cm single thread tapestry canvas, 18 threads (17 holes) to 2,5 cm, 68-cm wide.

50 cm matching medium weight fabric 91 cm wide for backing. Cushion pad to fit. Tapestry frame with 68 cm tapes. Milward International Range tapestry needle No. 18.

INSTRUCTIONS: Mark the centre of canvas lengthwise and widthwise with a line of basting stitches. Mount canvas in frame, long edges to tapes. *Diagram 1* gives one eighth of the complete design, centre indicated by black arrows which should coincide with the basting stitches. *Diagram 1* also shows the arrangement of the stitches on the threads of the canvas, represented by the background lines. The design is worked over 6 canvas threads throughout, except in those areas where the length of stitch has been adjusted to fit the diagonal corners and give a neat outer edge.

Commence the design centrally and work the foundation row following *diagram 1* for the design. Work the numbered sections with appropriate colour within each outlined shape. Continue working the remaining outer area 2 in 0842 only, following the stitch sequence. To complete one side, work the given eighth in reverse from the lengthwise arrow. To complete, turn canvas and work other three sides in the same way.

TO MAKE UP: Trim canvas to within 1,5 cm of embroidery. Cut a piece from backing fabric the same size. Place back and front right sides together and stitch close to the embroidery leaving an opening on one side for pad insertion. Turn to right side, insert pad, turn in seam allowance on open edges and slipstitch. **Diagram 2** shows a single row of stitches over 6 canvas threads.

Diagram 1

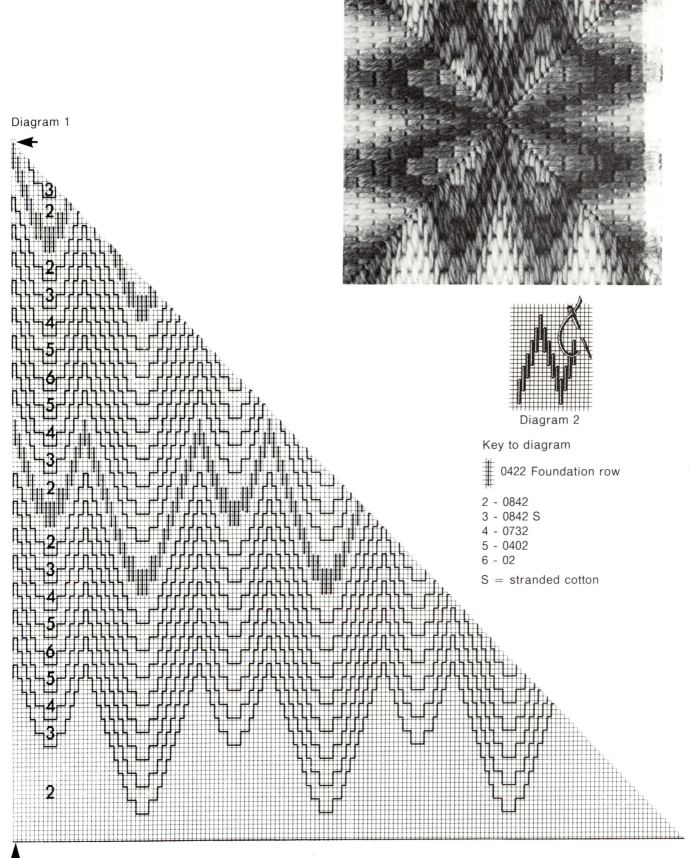

Diagram 2

Key to diagram

╫ 0422 Foundation row

2 - 0842
3 - 0842 S
4 - 0732
5 - 0402
6 - 02

S = stranded cotton

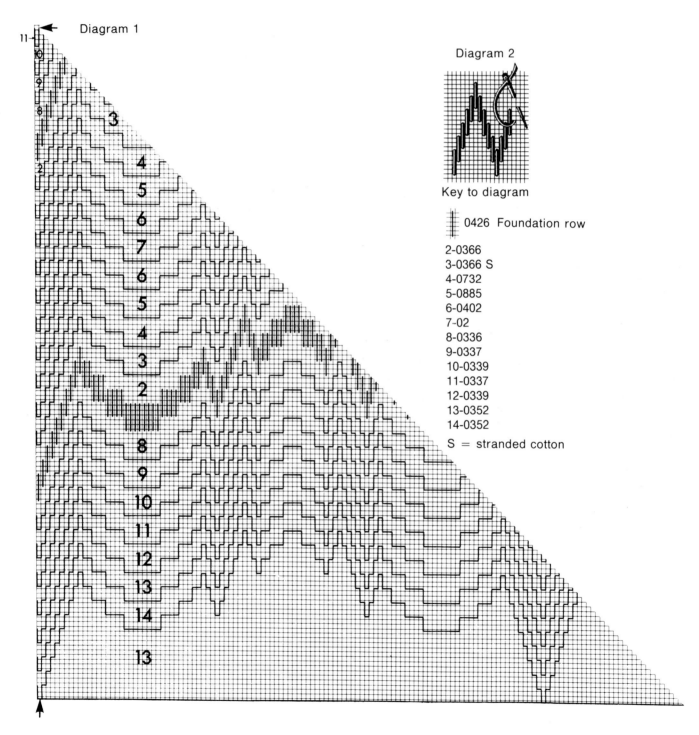

Diagram 1

Diagram 2

Key to diagram

▓ 0426 Foundation row

2-0366
3-0366 S
4-0732
5-0885
6-0402
7-02
8-0336
9-0337
10-0339
11-0337
12-0339
13-0352
14-0352

S = stranded cotton

Cushion

MATERIALS: Anchor Stranded Cotton: 3 skeins each terra cotta 0337, chestnut 0352; 2 skeins each cinnamon 0366, caramel 0885, brick red 0336; 1 skein cream 02. Use 6 strands throughout.

Anchor Tapisserie Wool (10 m skein): 9 skeins chestnut 0352; 2 skeins each peach 0426, 0366, brick red 0339, white 0402, cream 0732, nasturtium 0337 and terra cotta 0339.

50 cm single thread tapestry canvas 18 threads (17 holes) to 2,5 cm, 68 cm wide. 50 cm matching medium weight fabric 91 cm wide for backing. Cushion pad to fit. Tapestry frame with 68 cm tapes. Milward International Range tapestry needle No. 18.

INSTRUCTIONS: Mark the centre of canvas lengthwise and widthwise with a line of basting stitches. Mount canvas in frame, long edges to tapes. *Diagram 1* gives one eighth of the complete design, centre indicated by large black arrows which should co-incide with the basting stitches. *Diagram 1* also shows the arrangement of the stitches on the threads of the canvas, represented by the background lines. The design is worked over 6 canvas threads throughout, except in those areas where the length of stitch has been adjusted to fit the diagonal corners and give a neat outer edge.

Commence the design centrally and work the foundation row following *diagram 1*. Work the numbered sections with the appropriate colour. Continue working the remaining outer area 13 in 035 only, following the stitch sequence. To complete one side, work the given eighth in reverse from the lengthwise arrow. To complete, turn canvas and work other three sides in the same way.

TO MAKE UP: Trim canvas to within 1,5 cm of embroidery. Cut a piece from backing fabric the same size. Place back and front right sides together and stitch close to the embroidery leaving an opening on one side for pad insertion. Turn to right side, insert pad, turn in seam allowance on open edges and slipstitch.
Diagram 2 shows a single row of stitches over 6 canvas threads.

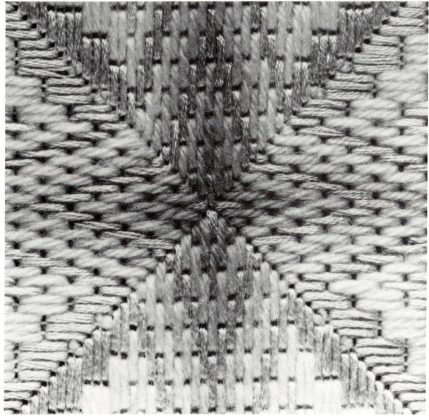

Velvet Cushion

MATERIALS: Coats Anchor Tapisserie Wool (10 m skein): 2 skein each peach 0366, 0570, white 0402, flesh pink 0421; 1 skein each haze 0497 sea grean 0505 and 0837.

43 cm × 43 cm piece evenweave fabric, 21 threads to 2,5 cm. 50 cm grey medium weight velvet 122 cm wide. 1,80 m matching cord. Cushion pad to fit. Square embroidery frame. Milward International Range tapestry needle No. 20.

INSTRUCTIONS: Cut a piece from velvet 43 cm × 43 cm. Mark the centre of evenweave fabric lengthwise and widthwise with a line of basting stitches. Place the evenweave fabric centrally on top of the velvet and base in position round edges. Mount fabric on frame. *Diagram 1*

gives an eighth of the design, centre indicated by blank arrow which should coincide with the vertical basting stitches. *Diagram 1* also shows the arrangement of the stitches on the threads of the fabric, represented by the background lines. The design is worked throughout over 8 fabric threads with the exception of the corners where it will be necessary to work part stitches to fit the diagonal.

Commence the design at small black arrow 129 threads down and 4 threads to the left of crossed basting stitches and work the foundation row, then the rest of embroidery following *diagram 1* and *key to diagram*. To complete one side, repeat in reverse to the left omitting centre stitch already worked. To complete design

turn fabric and work other three sides in the same way. On completion of embroidery remove from frame. Carefully unpick the basting stitches, trim away the evenweave fabric to within 2 cm of embroidery, then carefully withdraw all remaining fabric threads.

TO MAKE UP: Cut a piece from remaining velvet the same size as embroidered piece, for back. Place back and front right sides together raw edges even and baste and stitch 1,5 cm from edges leaving an opening on one side for pad insertion. Turn to right side, insert pad and sew open edges. Sew cord in position round edge.

Diagram 2 shows a single row of stitches over eight canvas threads.

Diagram 1

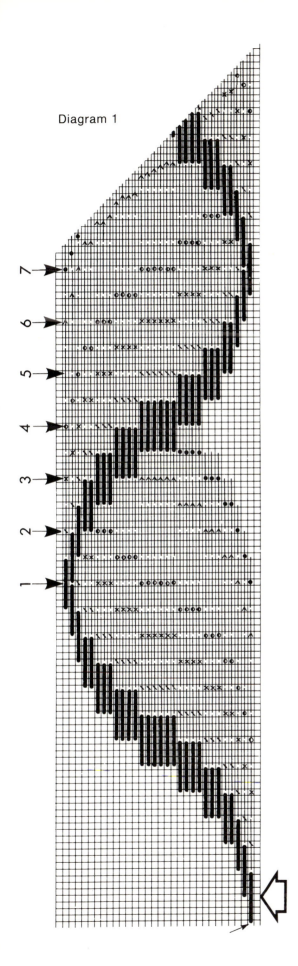

7

6

5

4

3

2

1

Diagram 2

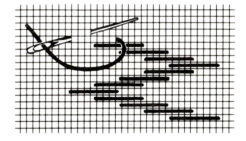

Key to diagram

1 - 0402 Foundation row
2 - 0366
3 - 0570
4 - 0421
5 - 0497
6 - 0837
7 - 0505

13

Cushion

MATERIALS: Anchor Tapisserie Wool (10 m skeins): 9 skeins mauve 096; 6 skeins each dusky pink 0892, cyclamen 067; 5 skeins lilac 0502; 4 skeins petrol blue 0848; 3 skeins Saxe Blue 0144; 2 skeins grey 0981.

50 cm single thread tapestry canvas 18 threads (17 holes) to 2,5 cm, 68 cm wide. 50 cm matching medium weight fabric 91 cm wide for backing. Cushion pad to fit. Tapestry frame with 68 cm tapes. Milward International Range tapestry needle No 18.

INSTRUCTIONS: Mark the centre of canvas lengthwise and widthwise with a line of basting stitches. Mount canvas in frame with long edges to tapes. *Diagram 1* gives one eighth of the complete design, centre indicated by black arrows which should coincide with the basting stitches. *Diagram 1* also shows the arrangement of the stitches on the threads of the canvas, represented by the background lines. The design is worked over 6 canvas threads throughout, except in those areas where the length of stitch has been adjusted to fit the diagonal corners and give a neat outer edge.

Commence the design centrally and work the foundation row following *diagram 1*. Work the numbered sections with appropriate colour. To complete one side, work the given eighth in reverse from the lengthwise arrow. To complete, turn canvas and work other three sides in the same way.

TO MAKE UP: Trim canvas to within 1,5 cm of embroidery. Cut a piece from backing fabric the same size. Place back and front right sides together and stitch close to the embroidery leaving an opening on one side for pad insertion. Turn to right side, insert pad, turn in seam allowance on open edges and slipstitch.

Diagram 2 shows a single row of stitches over 6 canvas threads.

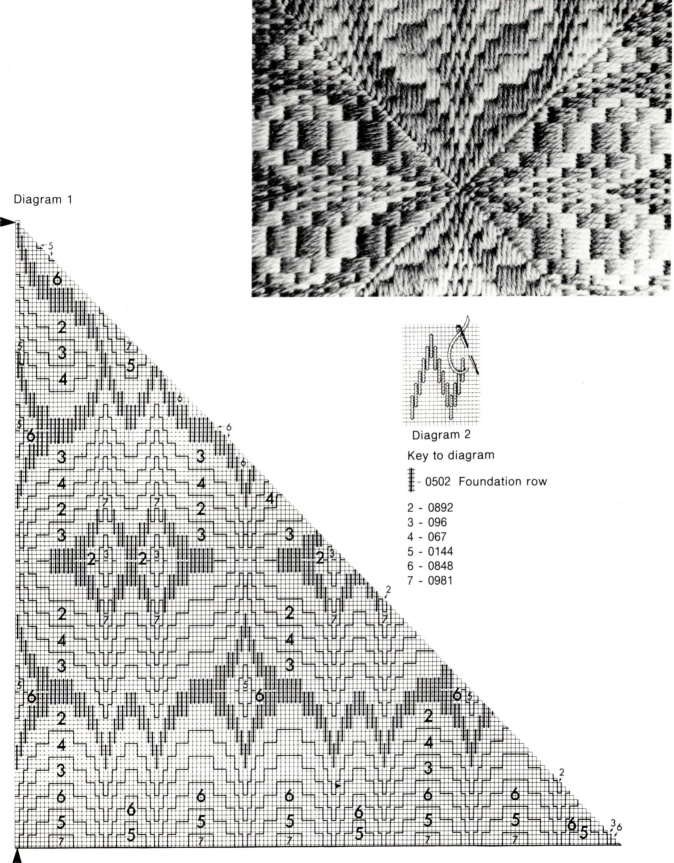

Diagram 1

Diagram 2

Key to diagram

▌ - 0502 Foundation row

2 - 0892
3 - 096
4 - 067
5 - 0144
6 - 0848
7 - 0981

Cushion

MATERIALS: Anchor Stranded Cotton: 5 skeins forest green 0264; 2 skeins jade 0189; 1 skein each jade 0187, apple green 0205, laurel green 0212, forest green 0267, emerald 0225, 0227 and parrot green 0257. Use 6 strands throughout.

30 cm single thread tapestry canvas 22 threads (21 holes) to 2,5 cm, 58 cm wide. 40 cm matching medium weight fabric 91 cm wide for front and back. Cushion pad to fit. Tapestry frame. Milward International Range tapestry needle No. 20.

INSTRUCTIONS: Cut a piece from canvas, 30 cm × 30 cm, and mark the centre both ways with a line of basting stiches. *Diagram 1* gives one eighth of the complete design, centre indicated by black arrows which should coincide with the basting stitches. *Diagram 1* also shows the arrangement of the stitches on the threads of the canvas, represented by the background lines. The design is worked throughout over 6 canvas threads, but it will be necessary to adjust the length of stitches to fit the diagonal corners and give a neat outer edge.

Commence the design centrally and work the foundation row 48 threads down from crossed basting stitches following *diagram 1* and key to diagram. Following pattern, work each numbered section in the appropriate colour, taking care to fill in area 7 in 0264 only. To complete one side, work the given eighth in reverse from the lengthwise basting stitches. Turn canvas and work other three sides in the same way.

TO MAKE UP: Trim canvas to within 1,5 cm of embroidery. Cut two pieces from fabric, 40 × 40 cm. Place the embroidery centrally to one piece of fabric and mark the outline of the finished edge of the embroidery with a line of basting stitches. Cut out centre section of fabric to within 1,5 cm of basting stitches, clipping fabric diagonally at the corners to the basting stitches. Fold back fabric at centre to the wrong side, place on top of embroidery and baste and edge stitch. Place back and front right sides together, baste and stitch 1,5 cm from edge on all sides leaving an opening on one side for pad insertion. Turn to right side, insert pad and sew open edges.

Diagram 2 shows a single row of stitches over 6 threads.

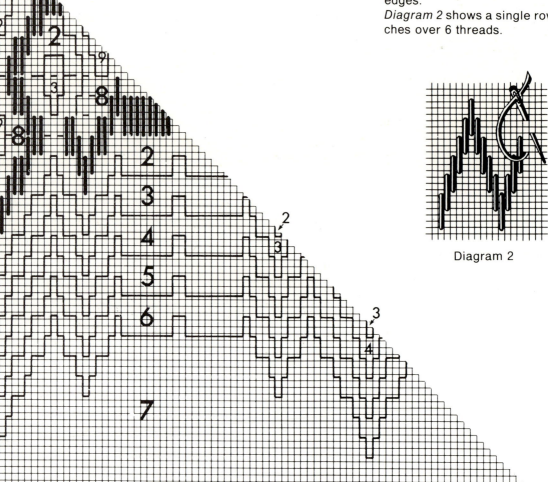

Diagram 1

Diagram 2

Key to diagram

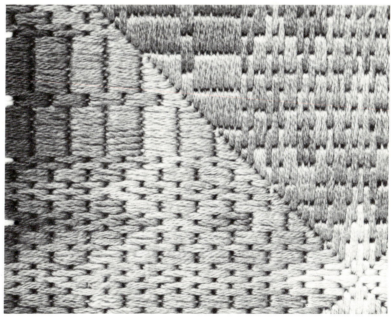

— 0187	Foundation row	

2 - 0225

3 - 0257

4 - 0227

5 - 0189

6 - 0212

7 - 0264

8 - 0205

9 - 0267

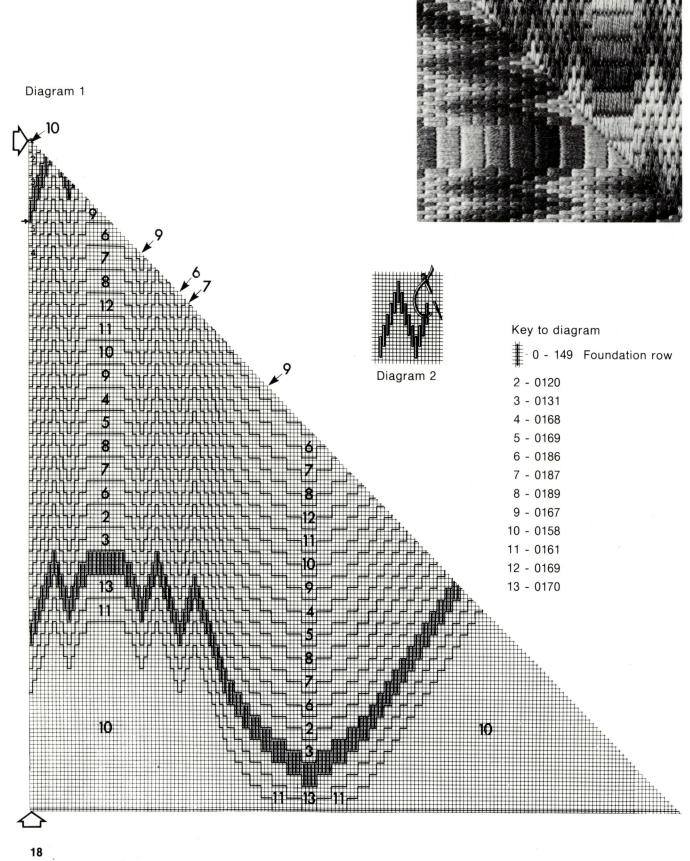

Diagram 1

Diagram 2

Key to diagram

0 - 149   Foundation row

2 - 0120
3 - 0131
4 - 0168
5 - 0169
6 - 0186
7 - 0187
8 - 0189
9 - 0167
10 - 0158
11 - 0161
12 - 0169
13 - 0170

Cushion

MATERIALS: Anchor Stranded Cotton: 15 skeins sea blue 0158; 4 skeins each jade 0186, 0187, 0189, sea blue 0161; 3 skeins cornflower 0149; 2 skeins each cornflower 0120, 0131, peacock blue 0168, 0169, turquoise 0167, sea blue 0169 and 0170. Use 6 strands throughout.

50 cm single thread canvas 22 threads (21 holes) to 2,5 cm, 58 cm wide. 50 cm matching medium weight fabric for backing, 91 cm wide. Tapestry frame with 68 cm tapes. Milward International Range tapestry needle No. 20.

INSTRUCTIONS: Mark the centre of canvas lengthwise and widthwise with a line of basting stitches. Mount canvas on frame long edges to tapes. *Diagram 1* gives an eighth of the design, centre indicated by blank arrows which should coincide with the basting stitches. *Diagram 1* also shows the arrangement of the stitches on the threads of the canvas represented by the background lines. The design is worked over 6 canvas threads throughout, except in those areas where the length of the stitch has been adjusted to fit the diagonal corners.

Commence the design centrally at small black arrow and work the foundation row. Work the numbered sections within each outlined shape with the colour, as given in key to diagram. To complete one side, work in reverse from the lengthwise arrow. In the outer areas 10 continue working in 0158 following the stitch sequence. To complete design turn the canvas and work other three sides in the same way.

TO MAKE UP: Trim canvas to within 1,5 cm of embroidery. Cut a piece from backing fabric the same size. Place back and front right sides together, raw edges even and baste and stitch close to embroidery on all sides leaving an opening for pad insertion. Turn to right side, insert pad and sew open edges.

Diagram 2 shows a single row of stitches over 6 threads.

Stooltop

MATERIALS: Stooltop approximately 74 × 29 cm. Adjust quantities to suit individual requirements.

Anchor Tapisserie Wool (10 m skein): 8 skeins each peach 0366, cream 0384, flesh pink 0421, haze 0497 and grey 0981

90 cm single thread tapestry canvas, 18 threads (17 holes) to 2,5 cm, 68 cm wide. Tapestry frame with 68 cm tapes. Milward International Range tapestry needle No. 18.

INSTRUCTIONS: Mark the centre of canvas widthwise and with a line of basting stitches. Mount canvas on frame with short edges to tapes. *Diagram 1* gives a section of the design, centre indicated by black arrows which should coincide with the basting stitches. *Diagram 1* also shows the arrangement of the stitches on the threads of the canvas represented by the background lines. The design is worked throughout over 6 canvas threads, but it will be necessary to work part stitches to fit the outline. The *lay-out diagram* gives a little more than the right half of the complete design, centre indicated by broken lines which should also coincide with the basting stitches. The shaded area represents the given section in *diagram 1*.

Commence the design centrally and work the foundation row following *diagram 1* and key to diagram. To complete the right half repeat the given section following the *lay-out diagram*. To complete the design work the left hand side to correspond.

TO MAKE UP: Place embroidery centrally on the stool pad. Fold canvas back and secure in position on the underside with upholstery tacks. *Diagram 2* shows a single row of stitches over 6 threads.

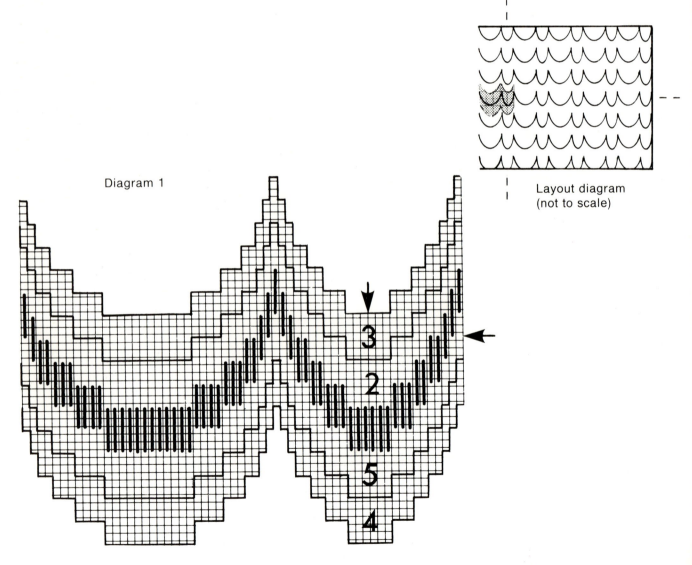

Diagram 1

Layout diagram
(not to scale)

20

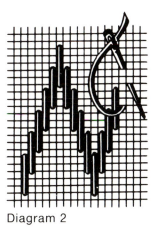

Diagram 2

Key to diagram

||| – 0497 Foundation
row

2 - 0384

3 - 0366

4 - 0421

5 - 0981

Cushion or stooltop

This attractive design is shown worked as a stooltop and a cushion. The materials are sufficient to work one of the articles. Working and making up instructions are given for the stooltop.

MATERIALS: Anchor Tapisserie Wool (10 m skein): 5 skeins haze 0497; 4 skeins white 0402; 2 skeins each raspberry 023, 024, salmon pink 0868 and 0740.

40 cm single thread tapestry canvas, 18 threads (17 holes) to 2,5 cm, 68 cm wide. Footstool approximately 27 × 21 cm. Tapestry frame with 46 cm tapes. Milward International Range tapestry needle No. 18.

INSTRUCTIONS: Cut a piece from canvas 45 cm × 40 cm and mark the centre lengthwise and widthwise with a line of basting stitches. Mount canvas in frame, long edges to tapes. *Diagram 1* gives a section of the design, centre indicated by blank arrows which should coincide with the basting stitches. *Diagram 1* also shows the arrangement of the stitches on the threads of the canvas, represented by the background lines. The design is worked throughout over 6 canvas threads, but it will be necessary to work part stitches to fit the outline shape. The *layout diagram* gives the complete design, centre indicated by broken lines which should also coincide with the basting stitches. The shaded area represents the given section in *diagram 1*.

Commence the design centrally and work the foundation row following *diagram 1* and key to diagram. To complete the design repeat the given section following the *layout diagram*.

TO MAKE UP: Place embroidery centrally on the stool pad. Fold the canvas to the back and secure in position on the underside with upholstery tacks.

Diagram 2 shows a single row of stitches over 6 threads.

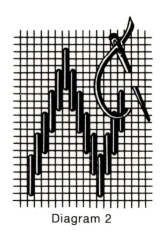

Diagram 2

Key to diagram
1 - 0402 Foundation row
2 - 024
3 - 023
4 - 0740
5 - 0868
6 - 0497

Layout diagram

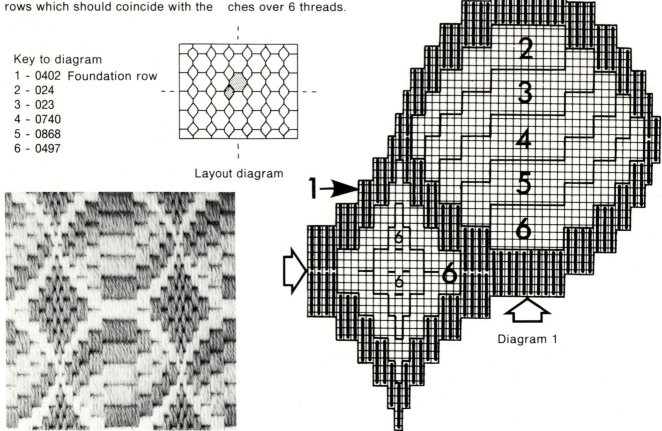

Diagram 1

Stooltop

MATERIALS: Stooltop approximately 52 × 30 cm. Quantities can be adjusted to suit individual requirements.

Anchor Tapisserie Wool (10 m skein): 5 skeins each peach 0366, cream 0729, flesh pink 0421, haze 0497 and grey 0390.

50 cm single thread tapestry canvas 18 threads (17 holes) to 2,5 cm, 68 cm wide. Tapestry frame with 68 cm tapes. Milward International Range tapestry needle No. 18.

INSTRUCTIONS: Mark the centre of canvas widthwise and lengthwise with basting stitches. With a soft pencil, draw an outline the required size centrally on the canvas. Mount the canvas in frame with long edges to tapes. *Diagram 1* gives a section of the design, centre indicated by black arrows which should coincide with the basting stitches. *Diagram 1* also shows the arrangement of the stitches on the threads of the canvas, represented by the background lines. The design is worked throughout over 6 canvas threads, but it will be necessary to work part stitches to fit the outline shape.

Commence the design centrally and work the foundation row across the canvas following *diagram 1* and key to diagram. Following the pattern, work each numbered section in the appropriate colour. To complete, continue working in this colour sequence to fill the outlined area.

TO MAKE UP: Place the embroidery centrally on the stool pad, fold the canvas back and secure in position on the underside with upholstery tacks.

Diagram 2 shows a single row of stitches over 6 canvas threads.

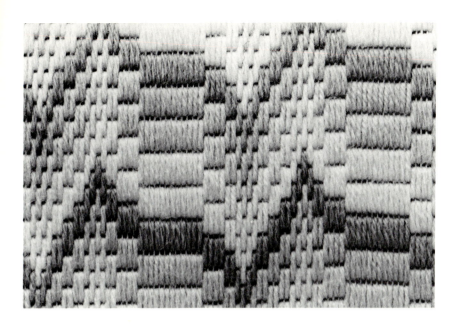

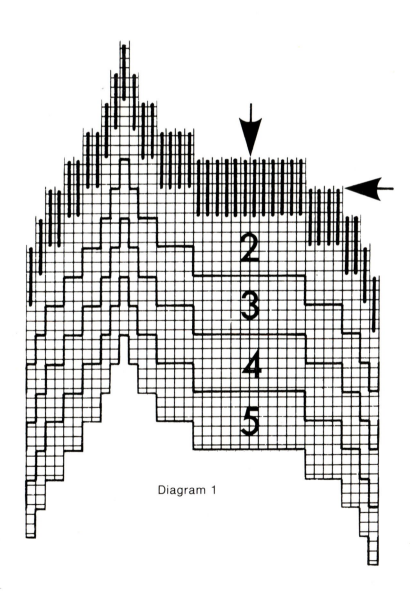

Diagram 1

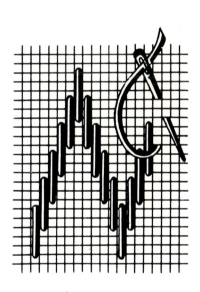

Diagram 2

Key to diagram

 – 0497 Foundation row

2 - 0390

3 - 0421

4 - 0366

5 - 0729

Cushion

Diagram 2

Key to diagram

⫴ - 0570 Foundation row

1 - 0366

2 - 0402

3 - 0847

4 - 0848

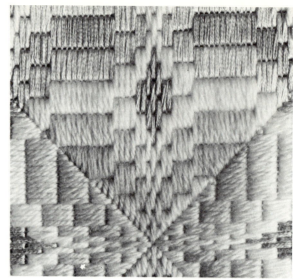

Diagram 1

MATERIALS: Coats Anchor Tapisserie Wool (10 m skein): 8 skeins white 0402; 6 skeins peach 0366; 3 skeins peach 0570. Anchor Stranded Cotton: 6 skeins each marine blue 0847, 0848. Use 6 strands throughout.

50 cm single thread tapestry canvas, 18 threads (17 holes) to 2,5 cm, 68 cm wide. 50 cm × 50 cm piece matching medium weight furnishing fabric (for backing cushion). Cushion pad to fit. Tapestry frame with 68 cm tapes. Milward International Range tapestry needle No. 18.

INSTRUCTIONS: Mark the centre of canvas lengthwise and widthwise with a line of basting stitches. Mount canvas on frame, long edges to tapes. *Diagram 1* gives an eighth of the design, centre indicated by blank arrows which should coincide with the basting stitches. *Diagram 1* also shows the arrangement of the stitches on the threads of the canvas, represented by the background lines. The design is worked throughout over 6 canvas threads, but it may be necessary to work part stitches to fit the outline shape.

Commence the design centrally with the foundation row and work following *diagram 1* and key for embroidery. To complete one quarter repeat in reverse to the left hand side omitting centre line already worked. To complete design, turn canvas and work other three quarters in the same way.

TO MAKE UP: Trim canvas to within 1,5 cm of embroidery. Cut a piece from backing fabric the same size and place to embroidery, right sides together, raw edges even. Baste and stitch close to embroidery, leaving an opening for pad insertion. Turn to right side, insert pad and sew open edges.

Diagram 2 shows a single row of stitches over 6 canvas threads.

Stooltop

MATERIALS: Stooltop 41 cm × 32,5 cm. It may be necessary to adjust quantities to suit individual requirements. Anchor Tapisserie Wool (10 m skeins): 6 skeins each grass green 0240, flesh pink 0421; 5 skeins each peppermint green 0569, Saxe Blue 0736; 4 skeins kingfisher 0161; 3 skeins apple green 0202; 2 skeins each Saxe Blue 0147, navy 0148 and jade 0187.

40 cm single thread canvas 18 threads (17 holes) to 2,5 cm, 68 cm wide. Tapestry frame with 68 cm tapes. Milward International Range tapestry needle No. 18.

INSTRUCTIONS: Mark the centre of canvas lengthwise and widthwise with a line of basting stitches. Mount canvas on frame, long edges to tapes.

Diagram 1 gives motifs A and B, centre indicated by black arrows which should coincide with the basting stitches. *Diagram 1* also shows the arrangement of the stitches on the threads of the canvas, represented by the background lines. The design is worked throughout over 6 canvas threads, but it will be necessary to work part stitches to fit the outline shape. The *layout diagram* gives a little more than the left half of the design, centre indicated by broken lines which should coincide with the bas-

ting stitches. The shaded area represents motifs A and B given in *diagram 1*.

Commence the design centrally and work the foundation row following *diagram 1* and key to diagram. To complete the left half repeat these motifs following *layout diagram*. To complete design, work the right half to correspond.

TO MAKE UP: Place the embroidery centrally on the stool pad. Fold the canvas back and secure in position on the underside with upholstery tacks.

Diagram 2 shows a single row of stitches over 6 threads.

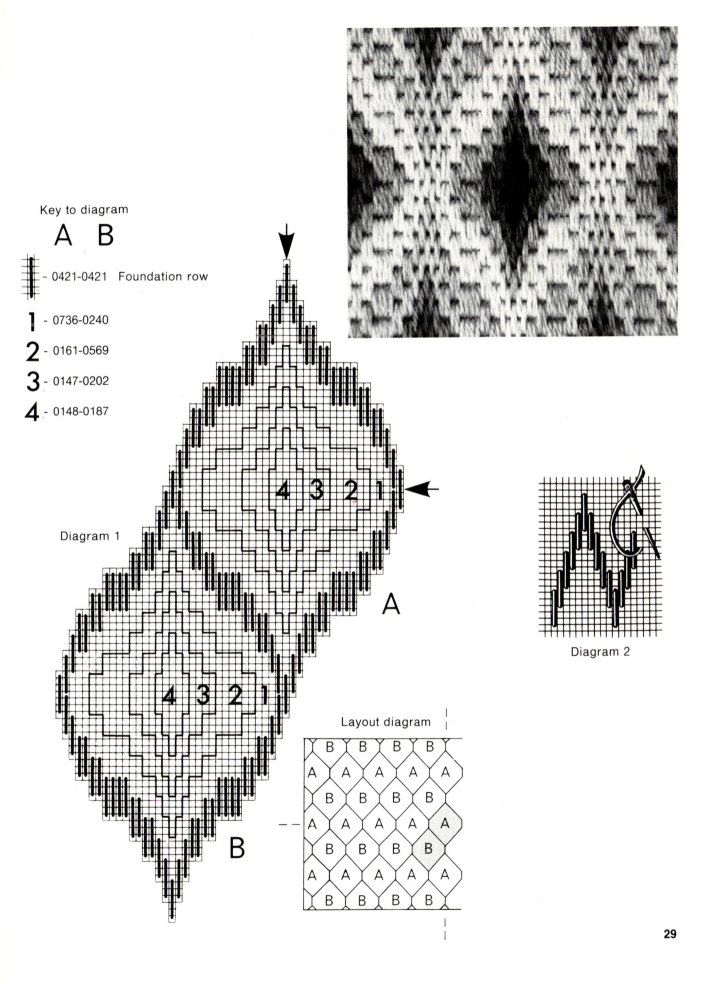

Key to diagram

A B

∦ - 0421-0421 Foundation row

1 - 0736-0240

2 - 0161-0569

3 - 0147-0202

4 - 0148-0187

Diagram 1

4 3 2 1

4 3 2 1

A

B

Diagram 2

Layout diagram

B	B	B	B
A	A	A	A	A
B	B	B	B
A	A	A	A	A
B	B	B	B
A	A	A	A	A
B	B	B	B

Stooltop

MATERIALS: Stooltop 41 × 32,5 cm. It may be necessary to adjust quantities to suit individual requirements. Anchor Tapisserie Wool (10 m skein): 3 skeins each raspberry 023, 024, 037, grass green 0240, moss green 0265, 0266, cinnamon 0358, salmon pink 0740, and moss green 0213.

40 cm single thread canvas 18 threads (17 holes) to 2,5 cm, 68 cm wide. Tapestry frame with 68 cm tapes. Milward International Range tapestry needle No. 18.

INSTRUCTIONS: Mark the centre of canvas lengthwise and widthwise with a line of basting stitches. Mount canvas on frame, long edges to tapes. *Diagram 1* gives motifs A and B, centre indicated by black arrows which should coincide with the basting stitches. *Diagram 1* also shows the arrangement of the stitches on the threads of the canvas, represented by the background lines. The design is worked throughout over 6 canvas threads, but it will be necessary to work part stitches to fit the outline shape. The *layout diagram* gives a little more than the left half of the design, centre indicated by broken lines which should coincide with the basting stitches. The shaded area represents motifs A and B given in *diagram 1*. Commence the design centrally and work the foundation row following *diagram 1* and key to diagram. To complete the left half repeat these motifs following *layout diagram*. To complete design work the right half to correspond.

TO MAKE UP: Place the embroidery centrally on the stool pad. Fold the canvas back and secure in position on the underside with upholstery tacks.

Diagram 2 shows a single row of stitches over 6 threads.

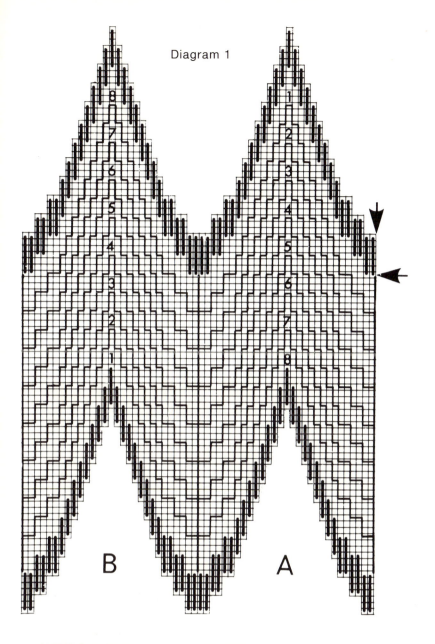

Diagram 1

8
7
6
5
4
3
2
1

1
2
3
4
5
6
7
8

B

A

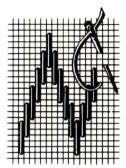

Diagram 2

Key to diagram

 - 0358 Foundation row

1 - 0266
2 - 0265
3 - 0240
4 - 0213
5 - 0740
6 - 023
7 - 024
8 - 037

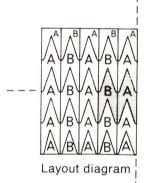

Layout diagram

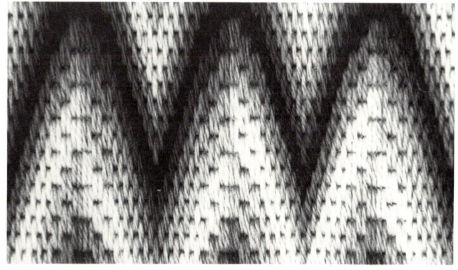

Delos 40 Heerengracht Cape Town
© 1989 J & P Coats
All rights reserved. No part of this book
may be reproduced or transmitted in any form
or any means without the written permission
of the publisher.
Set in 10 op 11 pt Helvetica Roman
by National Book Printers Goodwood
Printed by Nasionale Boekdrukkery
Goodwood
First impression, first print 1989

ISBN 1 86826 010 0